DINOSAUR WORLD

Contents

Published in 1982 by Rand McNally & Company

First published in 1981 by
Pan Books Ltd., London
Designed and produced by
Grisewood & Dempsey Ltd., London

Printed in Portugal
by Printer Portuguesa
Second printing 1983

Copyright © by Piper Books Ltd. 1981
U.S. edition © Piper Books Ltd. 1982

Library of Congress Catalog
Card No. 82 – 60155

DINOSAUR WORLD

David Lambert

Editor: Jacqui Bailey

Series Design: David Jefferis

RAND McNALLY & COMPANY
Chicago • New York • San Francisco

Before the Dinosaurs

Some of the largest animals that ever lived on land were dinosaurs. They ruled the world for many millions of years. Then they died out fast. What happened? Before we try to answer this, let's see how life began and then changed with time.

The world was very hot more than four billion years ago. When it cooled down, rain filled the oceans. There were still no living things on land. But life was starting in the oceans.

Sunshine and lightning gave off energy. This energy combined with chemicals. Tiny blocks of life were formed. **Bacteria** are very tiny plants. They may have been the first things made from these blocks of life. The bacteria ate food in the water. They ate it faster than it was being made. One kind of bacteria started to take in energy from sunlight. It made its own food from things in the air and water. Green plants developed from these bacteria. All animals eat plants or other animals. So after there were plants, there could be animals.

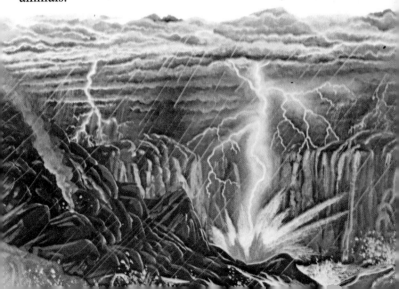

Life in Early Oceans

More than three billion years ago, living things were swimming in the oceans. Each of these early bacteria was one cell. Each early plant was one cell too. A cell like this is very small. A quarter of a million of them can fit on the head of a pin. When a cell of bacteria grows to a certain size, it splits. Then there are two.

Food and oxygen give power to a cell. If it grows too big, it can't take in enough oxygen and food. It can't get rid of waste. If it does not split, it might die.

Many Cells That Work as One

When cells join, they can form bigger living things. The largest whale is made of millions of cells. These cells are very small. We need a microscope to see them well.

The first groups of living cells were simple plants and animals. They lived about one billion years ago. They swam or held onto the seabed. Most simple plants and animals had offspring (young) like themselves. But some offspring were not just the same as their parents. And the next set of young was a little different too.

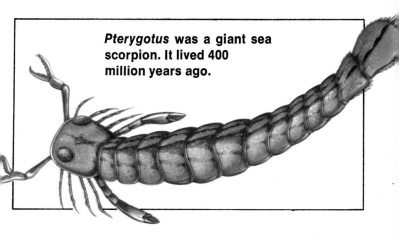

Pterygotus was a giant sea scorpion. It lived 400 million years ago.

After a while there were thousands of kinds of living things. They had to find food. They had to get away from enemies. Only those best at finding food and avoiding enemies survived and had young. Other kinds died out.

Some of the earliest living things: (1) sponges; (2) jellyfish; (3, 5, 14, 15) trilobites; (4) red algae; (6) *Aysheia*; (7) *Burgessia*; (8, 16) lamp shells; (9) *Emeraldella*; (10) corals; (11) *Waptia*; (12) *Marrella*; (13) green algae; (17) sea lilies; (18) echinoderms; (19) rag worm.

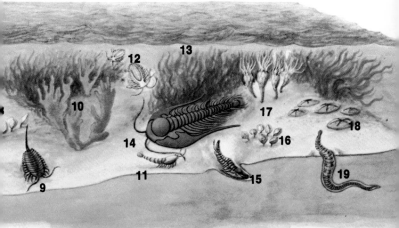

The First Fishes

Long ago one kind of sea animal had offspring. They had young. Some of the young that came much later were the first dinosaurs. But what kind of sea animal did dinosaurs come from?

Building with Bone

The jellyfish has a soft body. A jellyfish that is washed up on shore can't lift itself. It can't move on land. So dinosaurs could not have developed from jellyfish.

Crabs can walk on land. Their legs are jointed. Shells protect their bodies. As joint-legged animals grow, they must shed their shells. They have to grow bigger ones.

At first, a new shell is soft. The animal can't look for food or get away from enemies. It can't move around much until the shell grows harder. That's why animals with jointed legs could not have been the ancestors of dinosaurs.

Dinosaurs may have come from a creature related to today's sea squirt. Sea squirts have **notochords**. A notochord is a stiff rod inside the tail. Notochords were the start of **backbones**. A backbone is a strong rod made of bones. It has many joints.

Age of Fish

Fish were the first animals with backbones. There were very many fish from 345 to 395 million years ago. This was called the Age of Fishes.

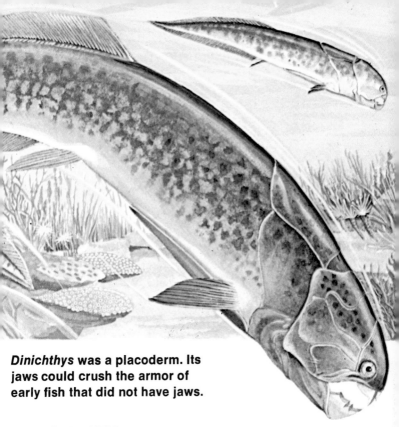

Dinichthys **was a placoderm. Its jaws could crush the armor of early fish that did not have jaws.**

Four Kinds of Fish

The first fish were small. They did not have jaws. Their mouths were just holes. These fish grubbed about in mud. They sucked in bits of food with water. Early fish that did not have jaws are called **ostracoderms**. Some fish without jaws developed from fish with jaws. One of these was the **placoderm**. Its head was protected by a hard cover that looked like armor. Some placoderms had jaws that could bite through the armor of other fish. A third kind of fish was **sharks** and **rays**. They were fish with soft cartilage (like the cartilage that our ears are made of). The fourth kind was the **bony fish**. We will discuss them in another section.

11

The First Land Plants

Fish were changing from one form to another. At the same time plants were growing on land. Sea animals could now come to the land. They would have plants to eat.

Land plants had two things that water plants did not have. The first was bright sunshine. This helped land plants make their food. Second, land plants got more oxygen. Living things need oxygen.

But many early plants were not suited to life on land. One early plant was seaweed. Seaweed made food by taking things from water. And seaweed does not have a stiff stem. It needs water to hold it up. It does not have roots that can take water and food from soil. The top parts of seaweed dry up quickly in the air.

From Algae to Forests

Tiny algae form green scum in ponds. Algae may have been the first plants to leave the water. By about 400 million years ago some algae had become plants that could live on land. *Cooksonia* is shown here. It was just a bunch of stems. It had no true roots. Club mosses were other early land plants. Later, ferns and horsetails came. They had roots to suck up minerals and water. Their stiff stems held their leaves up to the light. Tubes were inside the stems. These tubes took water to the leaves. They took food to the roots. Some club mosses and horsetails grew into tall trees. The Age of Fishes was the Age of the First Forests too.

The First Land Animals

Only a few land animals came from ocean animals. Most likely the first land animals came from **invertebrates**. Invertebrates are animals with no backbones. By 370 million years ago three groups of invertebrates lived on land. These groups are (1) some worms; (2) some **mollusks**; and (3) some **arthropods**. Mollusks are animals with soft bodies. Snails are mollusks. Arthropods are animals with jointed legs. Spiders and crabs are arthropods.

A cockroach feeds on things that are rotting. A scorpion hunts. Both lived in warm, wet forests more than 300 million years ago.

Insects and Spiders

Like worms, arthropods have soft, wet bodies. But an arthropod has a waterproof cover. Its legs are strong and jointed. So it does not need water to hold it up. Many arthropods could breathe dry air without drying their wet insides. Insects have tiny air holes in their outer skeletons. Air flows through these holes.

Millipedes and Hunters

Millipedes may have come from the first arthropods on land. They have many legs. They eat dead plants.

Hunters, such as centipedes and spiders, came after the millipedes. Soon there were more insects on land than any other animals. But as they grew, arthropods still had to lose the covers that kept them safe. That's why they could not grow very big on land.

Centipedes and millipedes have hard waterproof covers that keep their insides wet.

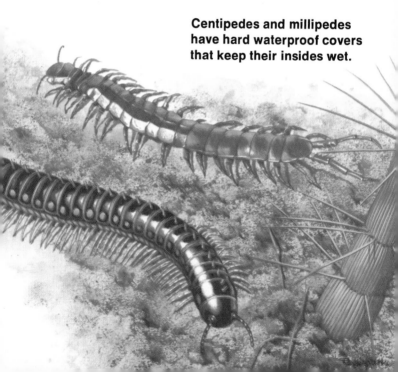

From Fins to Legs

Dinosaurs came from bony fish. All land animals with backbones came from bony fish. Most bony fish have bony rays. These rays hold up their fins. But one group had fins that grew from stubs of flesh. These were the **lobe-finned fish**. They were the first fish to move to land. The legs of all the land animals with backbones started with these lobes.

Three Groups of Lobe Fins

More than 345 million years ago there were three groups of lobe fins. **Coelacanths** (1) had strong stubs of fins. But coelacanths could not have breathed on land. Those that are alive now swim in the sea. **Lungfish** (2) had bags that worked as lungs. When pools dried up, early lungfish dug in mud. They breathed the same kind of air that we do. Today's lungfish do too.

Rhipidistians (3) ate flesh. Not one lives today. In the Age of Fishes there were many rhipidistians. They grew to be more than 3 yards (2.7 m) long. Like coelacanths, they had strong stubby fins. Like lungfish, they had lungs. Some swam in salt water. Others lived in fresh water. One kind that lived in fresh water was *Eusthenopteron*. The bones of its fins became the leg bones of land animals with backbones.

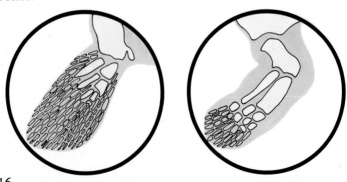

If their pool dried up, this fish could walk to another. If a big fish ran after baby *Eusthenopterons*, they could rush to shore. This fish spent part of its life on the banks of pools. Animals with backbones were beginning to come to land.

***Eusthenopteron* grabs another fish. Young *Eusthenopterons* may have gone to land to get away from parents' jaws.**

(Left to right) An amphibian's leg developed from a lobed fin. The drawings show what must have happened.

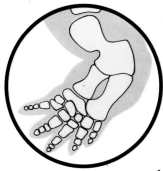

Amphibians Come

It was not easy for lobe fins to move about on land. But they were the ancestors of a group of animals that felt at home on land. These were **amphibians**. They had backbones. Today's frogs and salamanders are their relatives.

The First Amphibians

The first amphibian we know about was *Ichthyostega*. It was about 3 feet (90 cm) long. It was related to the lobe-finned fish. Its tail was like a lobe fin's. So were the roof bones of its skull. But a lobe fin had two fins. *Ichthyostega* had four legs instead. It had five toes on each foot. Its leg bones were strong. Its leg muscles were so strong it could walk.

In Hot, Wet Forests

A swamp is land that's full of water, like a wet sponge. Hot forests with swamps covered a lot of land about 300 million years ago. *Ichthyostega* or animals like it lived in these forests. These animals were the ancestors of many amphibians.

Many kinds of amphibians were **lepospondyls**. They were weak and skinny. Some swam like water snakes.

Most amphibians that lived long ago were **labyrinthodonts**. A labyrinth is a place with many halls. It's hard to find your way. Labyrinthodonts have hollow teeth that were like labyrinths. That's how labyrinthodonts got their name.

Some big labyrinthodonts had sharp, strong teeth. Sometimes they hunted on dry land.

They Needed Water

Many amphibians had to get their bodies wet sometimes. This stopped their skins from drying out.

Amphibians had soft, jellylike eggs without hard shells to keep the insides from drying out. So eggs were laid in the water.

Amphibians did not spend their entire lives on land. But they were the ancestors of backboned animals that did.

Lepospondyl amphibians:
Phlegethontia (left);
Ophiderpeton (center);
Microbrachis (right).

A fight between reptiles about 270 million years ago. *Dimetrodon* bites *Ophiacodon*'s neck.

The First Reptiles

About 290 million years ago, **reptiles** were formed from amphibians. Reptiles could stay on dry land all the time.

The first reptiles were small. Their bodies were near the ground. They looked like amphibians. But in four ways reptiles were not like amphibians: (1) reptiles' skins had scales and were waterproof; (2) their eggs had tough or hard shells that kept the eggs from drying out; (3) reptiles could run—they had the kind of leg bones needed for running; (4) their blood and the way they breathed gave them energy to run.

More and More Reptiles

Deserts replaced forest swamps. There were not so many amphibians. There were more and more reptiles. By 250 million years ago there were reptiles of many shapes and sizes.

Here *Dimetrodon* babies hatch from their eggs. Amphibians lay soft eggs, like jelly. Reptiles lay eggs with a tough or hard shell. The shell is waterproof. Shells like this hold food and water. They keep eggs from drying out.

"Terrible Lizards"

Dinosaurs came about 205 million years ago. They developed from reptiles. The word *dinosaur* means "terrible lizard."

Skeletons of dinosaurs look like lizards' skeletons. But people who study dinosaurs don't think they were reptiles. Reptiles are cold-blooded. Cold-blooded animals stay as warm or as cold as the air and water around them. People think dinosaurs were warm-blooded like humans. That is, the heat of their bodies always stayed about the same.

How Dinosaurs Began

The first dinosaurs came from reptiles that swam. These reptiles hunted for animals in water. *Euparkeria* came from these first reptiles. *Euparkeria* was like a small crocodile with long legs. *Euparkeria* lived on land.

There were two main groups of dinosaurs. One group had hips like birds'

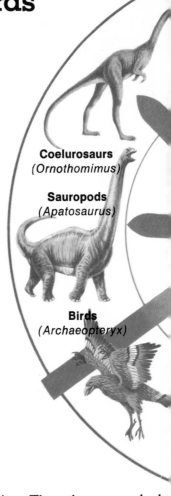

Coelurosaurs
(Ornothomimus)

Sauropods
(Apatosaurus)

Birds
(Archaeopteryx)

hips. The other group had hips like those of lizards. Most likely, *Euparkeria* and its relatives were the ancestors of both groups.

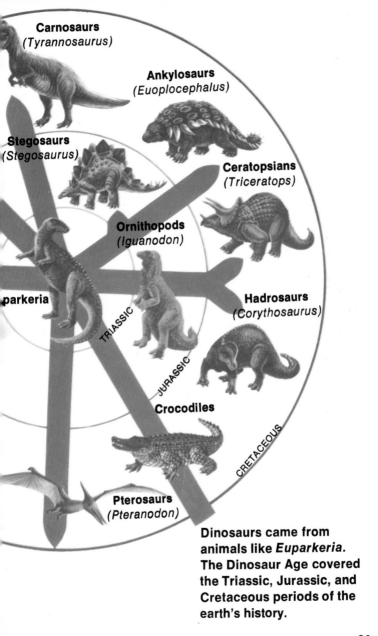

Carnosaurs
(*Tyrannosaurus*)

Ankylosaurs
(*Euoplocephalus*)

Stegosaurs
(*Stegosaurus*)

Ceratopsians
(*Triceratops*)

Ornithopods
(*Iguanodon*)

parkeria

Hadrosaurs
(*Corythosaurus*)

TRIASSIC

JURASSIC

Crocodiles

CRETACEOUS

Pterosaurs
(*Pteranodon*)

Dinosaurs came from animals like *Euparkeria*. The Dinosaur Age covered the Triassic, Jurassic, and Cretaceous periods of the earth's history.

23

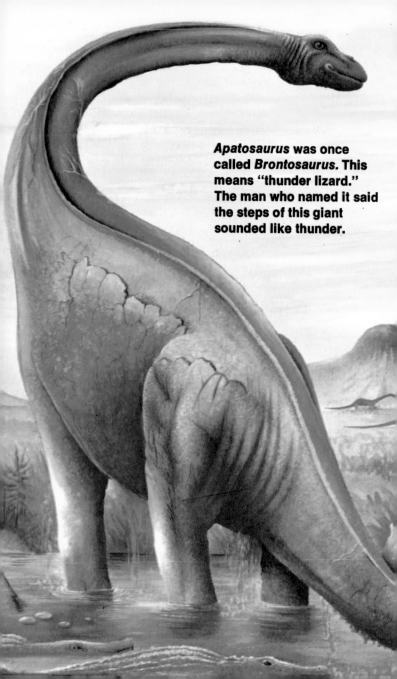

Apatosaurus was once
called *Brontosaurus*. This
means "thunder lizard."
The man who named it said
the steps of this giant
sounded like thunder.

The Giants

Some **lizard-hipped dinosaurs** were the biggest animals that ever lived on land. People who study about these giants call them **sauropods**. Sauropods means "feet like lizards."

These dinosaurs had huge bodies. They had legs like tree trunks. They had small heads, long necks, and long tails. The biggest sauropod may have been taller than a seven-story building.

Sauropods were big and strong. But they did not hurt other animals. They ate the plants that grew in the warm forests.

Brachiosaurus was the biggest of these five. **Diplodocus** was the longest dinosaur of all.

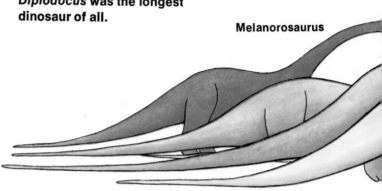

Melanorosaurus

A World of Monsters

There were more and more dinosaurs. Many kinds went to other parts of the world. Most likely sauropods came from *Ticinosuchus*. *Ticinosuchus* was a reptile. It was a relative of *Euparkeria*. *Ticinosuchus* walked on four legs. It was more than 3 yards (2.7 m) long. It was the ancestor of sauropods like *Melanorosaurus*. The sauropod was as long as seven people lying head to toe. Sauropods that came later were even larger. *Apatosaurus* grew as long as fourteen people lying head to toe. Another name for *Apatosaurus* was *Brontosaurus*.

Super Giants

The longest land animal was *Diplodocus*. This animal grew to be almost 30 yards (27 m) long. Another giant, *Brachiosaurus*, weighed as much as twenty elephants.

In 1972 people found what was left of a bigger monster. It may have weighed as much as fifty big elephants. They gave it the nickname *Supersaurus*. It was found in Colorado.

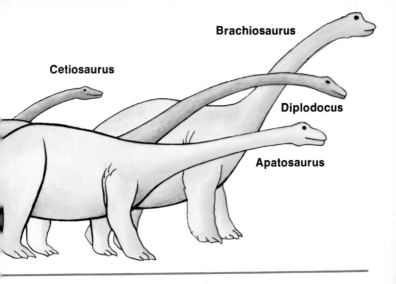

Cetiosaurus

Brachiosaurus

Diplodocus

Apatosaurus

They Had to Be Big

Sauropods were big. Their size helped keep them alive. Bodies of big cold-blooded animals cool down slower than bodies of small ones. If sauropods were cold-blooded, their size helped keep their bodies warm. And they were so big, they could kill all but their biggest enemies.

Maybe sauropods had to be big to eat enough plants to survive. Some sauropods ate half a ton of leaves a day! But their teeth couldn't grind leaves. Their stomachs had to grind them. Sauropods may have swallowed little stones. These helped crush the leaves. So a sauropod needed a very big stomach. And it needed a very big body to hold that stomach.

How They Lived

Sauropods had long necks like giraffes. They could find food in the tops of trees. Sauropods roamed in herds. This helped protect them from enemies.

An *Allosaurus* (right) runs after a *Coelurus* (left) in North America 150 million years ago. Other dinosaurs are eating plants.

Hunters on Two Legs

Even when sauropods ate, they watched for enemies. Their biggest enemies were **theropods**. A theropod had two legs. There were two groups of theropods.

Like Birds

One group of theropods looked like birds. They were

coelurosaurs. They were named for *Coelurus*. This dinosaur was longer than a person. But it did not weigh as much. It ran fast on its long back legs. It put its neck out in front. Its long tail kept it from falling over. Most likely, *Coelurus* hunted lizards and small mammals. It may have hunted birds.

Fangs

Sauropods also had to watch out for bigger theropods. These were the **carnosaurs**. Carnosaurs ate flesh. The most terrible carnosaur was *Allosaurus*. *Allosaurus* was about 13 yards (11.7 m) long. It walked on its two back legs. It had sharp claws. Its teeth were like knives. *Allosaurus* hunted sauropods of North America about 150 million years ago.

The Cruel King

Tyrannosaurs were the most cruel carnosaurs. *Tyrannosaur* means "tyrant lizard." A tyrant is a cruel ruler. Tyrannosaurs lived late in the Dinosaur Age.

The carnosaur we know best is *Tyrannosaurus rex*. The name means "king of the tyrant lizards." *Tyrannosaurus* lived in North America about 70 million years ago.

Weapons

Tyrannosaurus was about 15 yards (13.5 m) long. If it were alive today, it could look in our upstairs windows. Its

Tyrannosaurus had huge jaws. This carnosaur ate the dinosaurs that lived on plants.

back toes had claws. They were like knives used to carve meat. Its fangs were as long as a person's hand. They lined its jaws. But the arms of *Tyrannosaurus* were tiny. They were too small to be used as weapons. They were too short to bring food to *Tyrannosaurus's* mouth.

An *Ornithomimus* steals the eggs another dinosaur laid.

Ostrich Dinosaurs

A dinosaur laid eggs in the sand. *Struthiomimus* came along. It wanted the eggs. Maybe it used its hands to scoop away the sand. Its claws may have smashed the eggs open.

Coelurosaurs were like birds. The largest coelurosaurs lived late in the Dinosaur Age. They looked like ostriches that had lost their feathers. They had long legs and long tails. They had "hands." These hands had claw tips. Coelurosaurs may have used their hands to steal other dinosaurs' eggs.

Fast Runners

If an enemy came near, an ostrich dinosaur ran away. Most likely it could run as fast as an ostrich. That is about 48 miles (77 km) an hour. Only warm-blooded animals can go that fast. So it seems coelurosaurs were not cold-blooded reptiles.

Bird-Hipped Dinosaurs

Both of the biggest dinosaurs were lizard-hipped. But many **bird-hipped dinosaurs** were very big too. All bird-hipped dinosaurs ate plants. Some walked on two legs. Others moved on four legs. *Fabrosaurus* was one of the first bird-hipped dinosaurs. It was no bigger than a large lizard.

Fabrosaurus stood on long back legs like a flesh eater. But *Fabrosaurus* was a plant eater. Its beak and teeth were made for cutting and grinding leaves. It lived in southern Africa.

Bird-Footed Dinosaurs

Dinosaurs that had feet like birds are called **ornithopods**. One of the largest ornithopods was *Iguanodon*. *Iguanodon* got its name because of its teeth. They looked like the teeth of today's iguana lizards.

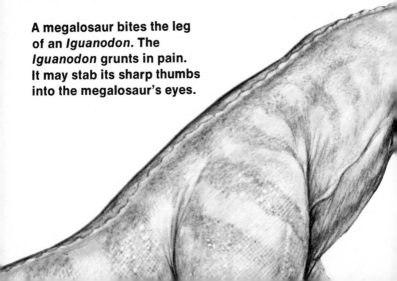

A megalosaur bites the leg of an *Iguanodon*. The *Iguanodon* grunts in pain. It may stab its sharp thumbs into the megalosaur's eyes.

Duckbills

The Dinosaur Age was almost over. In the north there were more and more relatives of *Iguanodon*. We call them **hadrosaurs**. This means "big lizards." They were about 10 yards (9 m) long. This was about as long as *Iguanodon*. But hadrosaurs did not weigh as much as *Iguanodon*.

Hadrosaurs walked on big back legs. The legs had three toes. Each arm had four fingers with webs.

Beaks

The head of a hadrosaur was very strange. It was long. The jaws of hadrosaurs were flat and wide. They looked like the jaws of ducks. Hadrosaurs were nicknamed "duckbills." Some kinds of hadrosaurs had as many as two thousand teeth.

People used to think a hadrosaur lived like a duck. They said the hadrosaurs' flat tails helped them swim.

But people who study dinosaurs looked at what was left of one hadrosaur's body. They found bits of what had once been leaves, fruit, and seeds.

Duckbills lived on land. They used their beaks to cut leaves. They mashed these with their many teeth.

Strange Tops

Duckbills had long bones that grew out of the tops of their heads. These strange bones are called **crests**. Different kinds of duckbills had different kinds of crests. *Kritosaurus* had a crest above its nose.

Parasaurolophus had a horn. It curved back from the top of the head. *Corythosaurus* had a tall round crest.

People who study duckbills think these bones helped hadrosaurs know their own kind.

These are dinosaurs with duck bills. They are *Parasaurolophus.* They are getting their food from trees of the forest.

Boneheads

Boneheaded dinosaurs were as strange as duckbills. Boneheads did not have bones growing out of their heads. But their skulls were *very* thick.

Yaverlandia was a dinosaur with bird hips and bird feet. It had two thick bony places above its eyes. *Yaverlandia* was about the size of a turkey. It had a long tail. When it walked, its tail was straight out. From *Yaverlandia* came bigger boneheads with thicker skulls.

Large and Small

The bonehead *Stegoceras* was the size of a human. But its brain was the size of a hen's egg. Thick bone covered its brain. This bone was five times as thick as a human's skull.

Pachycephalosaurus had a much bigger skull. *Pachycephalosaurus* means "reptile with a thick head." This dinosaur was the biggest bonehead of all. Its brain was small. Its skull was twenty times thicker than a human's. The skull of *Pachycephalosaurus* was three times as long as the skull of *Stegoceras*. Lumps of bone made the back of the skull extra strong. Spikes of bone pointed up from the dinosaur's nose.

Built-In Crash Helmets
Maybe the thick skulls kept the animals' brains from being hurt in fights.

Sometimes two male *Pachycephalosaurus* dinosaurs would fight. They fought over a certain mate. They fought about which one would lead the herd of boneheads. Most likely they did not fight to kill. Their heads crashed together. Their backbones shook. But their small brains were safe.

Dinosaurs with Armor

Some bird-hipped dinosaurs walked on four legs. They could not run away from their enemies. Their legs were too short. But parts of their bodies protected them.

Giants

Long ago, fighters wore suits of armor. These suits were made of metal plates. This armor protected their bodies.

Millions and millions of years before that, dinosaurs had their own armor. Some had plates of bone. These protected their bodies. Others had big horns.

Stegosaurs were the first dinosaurs with armor. *Stego-saurs* means "reptiles with plates."

The first stegosaur we know about was *Scelido-saurus*. It was as long as a car. Its hips were higher than its shoulders. Its head was small.

A stegosaur had bony bumps along its back. These helped keep it safe.

Scelidosaurus lived in southern England 190 million years ago.

Stegosaurus

Stegosaurus was much bigger than *Scelidosaurus*. Its armor was much better. *Stegosaurus* had two rows of bony plates. They grew out of its back. These plates were wide and had points at the ends.

Stegosaurus had a small head. Its brain was about the size of a walnut!

Stegosaurus walked over lands of the north about 150 million years ago. It died out. We don't know why. Most likely carnosaurs ate *Stegosaurus*.

Dinosaurs with more armor came next.

The bony plates of *Stegosaurus* may have let out heat to cool its body. To warm up, the plates may have caught heat from the sun.

More Armor

Many animals that ate flesh had claws and fangs. Sometimes these cut between the plates of plated dinosaurs. Most likely that's why plated dinosaurs died out.

The next dinosaurs had more armor. Their ribs were curved. So they were called **ankylosaurs**. *Ankylosaurs* means "rounded reptiles."

Ankylosaurs were long and low. They had bony plates, spikes, or lumps covering most of their bodies.

Early Ankylosaurs
Two kinds of ankylosaurs roamed southern England. One was *Acanthopholis*. It was about 4 yards (3.6 m) long. It had flat bony plates on its back and tail.

Acanthopholis could bend its back because of the way its plates were joined.

Another of the first ankylosaurs was *Polacanthus*. It was longer than *Acanthopholis*. It had rows of tall spikes to protect itself. They

pointed up from its head to halfway down its back.

Later Ankylosaurs
After the early ankylosaurs came animals with even better armor. One of these was *Euoplocephalus*. It lived in North America. It was two times as heavy as *Stegosau-*

rus. But it was only half as long.

Euoplocephalus had plates on its head, neck, and back. The plates had sharp edges. The tail ended in a bony club.

Scolosaurus was even harder to attack. Bony plates and sharp spikes covered its top and sides.

(Above) *Euoplocephalus* was about the size of a car. (Below) Carnosaurs would have their teeth snapped off if they bit into *Euoplocephalus*.

They Lived Long

The only part of an ankylosaur that could be hurt easily was its belly. But an ankylosaur was low on the ground. Only a few animals could turn it upside down. That's why ankylosaurs lived until the end of the Dinosaur Age.

Dinosaurs with Horns

Sometimes carnosaurs tried to fight dinosaurs that had armor. Most of them did not fight back. But dinosaurs that had horns *did* fight.

Parrot Reptiles

Psittacosaurus was the ancestor of dinosaurs with horns. Its name means "parrot lizard."

Psittacosaurus had two legs. Its beak was like a parrot's beak. It cut leaves from plants that had flowers.

Psittacosaurus was the size of a human. Most likely this kind of dinosaur was the ancestor of *Protoceratops*. *Protoceratops* means "first face with horns."

Protoceratops walked on four legs. It weighed more than one and a half tons.

Horns

A family of much larger dinosaurs came from *Protoceratops*. Many of them had a set of long bony bumps. These bumps protected their backs. Most of these dinosaurs had horns. The horns stuck out above their eyes.

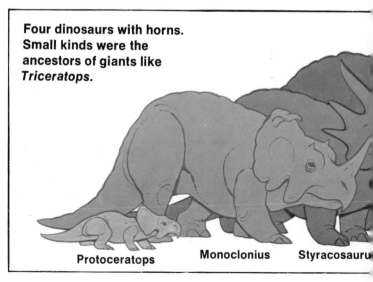

Four dinosaurs with horns. Small kinds were the ancestors of giants like *Triceratops*.

Protoceratops   Monoclonius   Styracosauru

Triceratops

(Above) *Triceratops* **cut off leaves with its beak. It sliced them with its sharp teeth.**

The biggest of all the dinosaurs with horns was *Triceratops*. Its name means "face with three horns." *Triceratops* was about 12 yards (10.8 m) long. It weighed eight and a half tons. Of all the dinosaurs only the sauropods were bigger. Most likely even *Tyrannosaurus* ran from *Triceratops*.

The Dinosaurs' World

All dinosaurs needed other living things. The biggest dinosaurs ate plants. Big flesh-eating dinosaurs ate other dinosaurs. Most of the smaller dinosaurs ate reptiles, birds, and mammals.

Dinosaurs have died out. Many of the plants and animals they ate have died out too. But they fit in well with the world of their time. This chapter is about animals and plants that shared the dinosaurs' world.

That world was not like ours. Before the dinosaurs, all continents were one big land. In the Dinosaur Age that land was breaking up. This happened slowly. Many dinosaurs and other land animals had time to spread to lands that are now separated by oceans. The lands were very hot. Even places that are the coldest now were warm then.

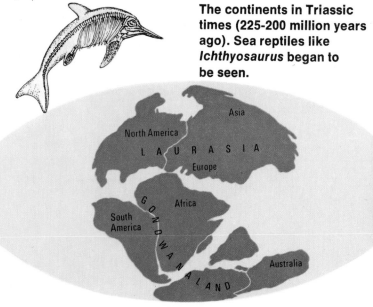

The continents in Triassic times (225-200 million years ago). Sea reptiles like *Ichthyosaurus* began to be seen.

Asia

North America

L A U R A S I A

Europe

Africa

South America

G O N D W A N A L A N D

Australia

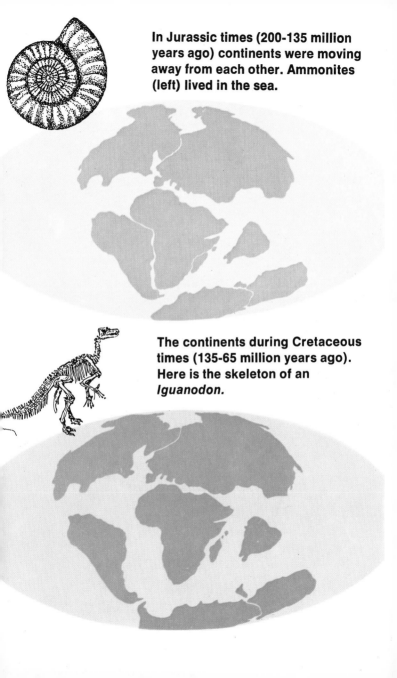

In Jurassic times (200-135 million years ago) continents were moving away from each other. Ammonites (left) lived in the sea.

The continents during Cretaceous times (135-65 million years ago). Here is the skeleton of an *Iguanodon.*

Early Plants

Before dinosaurs moved over the land, plants were there. Dinosaurs needed plants.

Early land plants grew from tiny dots called **spores**. These spores needed wet soil so they wouldn't dry out. It is good that dinosaurs didn't come sooner. They would have had to live in swamps and next to rivers. When the Dinosaur Age began, many swamps had dried up. But there were new plants that could live on dry land.

Plants from the Dinosaur Age. Some of them are ginkgos, swamp cypress, ferns, tree ferns, and horsetails.

Naked Seeds

The new land plants made spores. Large spores stayed on the parent plant. Small spores blew away and became pollen. Pollen landed on a large spore. The pollen fertilized it. The spore became a seed.

Trees that grew from seeds like these are: (1) **cyclads**, which are like palms, and (2) **conifers**, which have cones. Both of these trees have seeds that are not covered all over. These trees are called **gymnosperms**. This means "naked seeds." Gymnosperms grew in the Dinosaur Age.

Capsule Seeds

When the Dinosaur Age was about half over, plants with flowers started to grow. Fruit or a small cover protected the seeds. This small cover is called a capsule. That's why plants with flowers are called **angiosperms**. It means "capsule seeds."

When the Dinosaur Age ended, there were many plants with flowers.

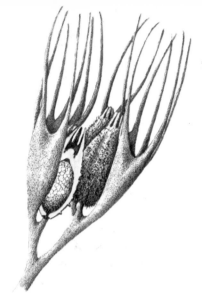

(Above) The oldest seed we know about came from a plant that grew 390 million years ago. A leaf bract protected it. (Below) The cone of today's conifer.

The First Mammals

Small animals with fur ran away from dinosaurs walking around. These animals looked like shrews or mice. They were warm-blooded. They were the first **mammals**. Mammals came from reptiles.

A mammal family eats an insect. A dinosaur is above them. It's so big it can't see them.

Reptiles are cold-blooded. They stay as warm as the air or water around them. Reptiles move around only when the air is warm. They don't have hair. They have scales. Their legs are short.

Strange Reptiles and Early Mammals

When the Dinosaur Age began, there were strange reptiles in the world. Many had legs below their bodies, not at their sides. Some may have been warm-blooded.

Dinosaurs killed most of the reptiles that were like mammals. One small kind lived long enough to develop into mammals.

Early mammals hunted insects. Most likely these mammals laid eggs. But they fed their babies milk from special glands. They could control the heat of their bodies. So they could move around in the cold.

These mammals were too small to fight dinosaurs.

Lizards and Snakes

When the Dinosaur Age was starting, there were many new kinds of reptiles. Most of them lived on land. Some died out long ago. Others live today.

Lizards That Glide

Lizards are one of the oldest groups of reptiles still living. Some of the earliest lizards are like the gliding lizards of today. A gliding lizard has long ribs. It lives high in the trees. When it jumps into the air, it spreads its ribs. It has a flap of skin on each side of its body. The flaps act like a parachute.

The lizard *Kuehneosaurus* lived long ago. Most likely it glided in the same way as today's gliding lizards. The picture shows *Kuehneosaurus*.

Odd Lizards

Lizards were the ancestors of some other reptiles. One reptile was the strange animal, *Tanystropheus*. It had a long neck. There was also a group of large swimming "lizards" called **mosasaurs**.

But most lizards of long, long ago were small and shy. They ate insects as most lizards do now. When a dinosaur came by, they hid.

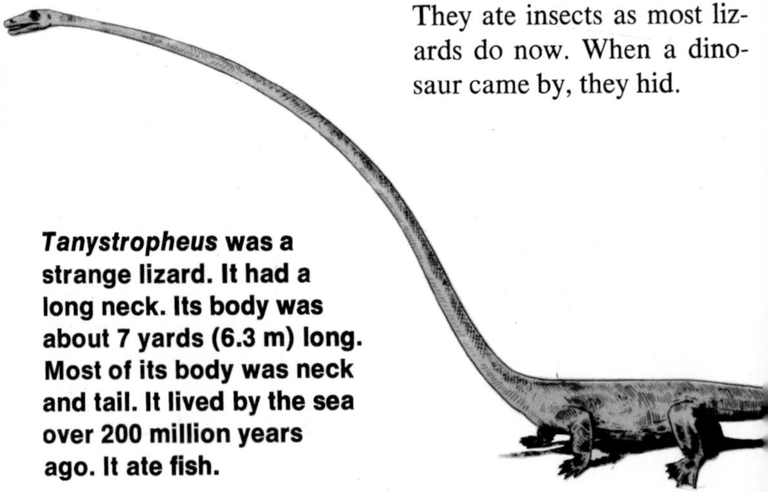

Tanystropheus was a strange lizard. It had a long neck. Its body was about 7 yards (6.3 m) long. Most of its body was neck and tail. It lived by the sea over 200 million years ago. It ate fish.

The First Snakes

When the Dinosaur Age was ending, snakes appeared. They came from lizards. These reptiles had no legs. They looked like the pythons of today. Pythons are strong snakes. They coil around their prey. Then the prey can't breathe. It dies.

Beakheads

The tuatara is the strangest reptile alive today. It is the only **beakhead** still living. The upper jaw of a beakhead looks like a beak.

The animals we call **rhynchosaurs** were beakheads. They were about 2 yards (1.8 m) long. They had flat plates inside their huge jaws. When there were many dinosaurs, rhynchosaurs died out.

53

Wings of Skin

Pterosaurs came from the group of reptiles that led to dinosaurs. Pterosaurs were masters of the air. Their name means "lizards with wings." They came from gliding reptiles. They must have looked like the gliding lizards we have talked about.

By 200 million years ago many kinds of pterosaurs were developing. Their bones were thin, hollow, and light. The wings were skin. They curved to the back legs.

Many pterosaurs had weak muscles. They could not flap their wings. So they glided. They steered well. Their jaws were long and shaped like beaks. Pterosaurs glided low to grab fish or lizards.

Pterosaurs' legs were very short. That's why pterosaurs could not get around very well on land. They slept in treetops where enemies could not get them.

Beaks with Points

A prow is the front part of a ship. It is pointed. The first group of pterosaurs had beaks like prows. That's why they were called "prow beaks." **Prow beaks** steered with their long tails. They had sharp teeth. Their wings were short and wide.

Maybe all pterosaurs had fur. One prow beak has been named "hairy devil."

Some people who study the pterosaur think it was warm-blooded. They say that's why it had energy to fly.

The second group of pterosaurs were **pterodactyloids**.

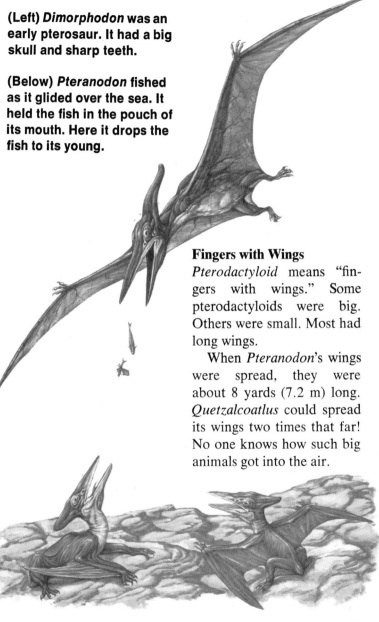

(Left) *Dimorphodon* was an early pterosaur. It had a big skull and sharp teeth.

(Below) *Pteranodon* fished as it glided over the sea. It held the fish in the pouch of its mouth. Here it drops the fish to its young.

Fingers with Wings

Pterodactyloid means "fingers with wings." Some pterodactyloids were big. Others were small. Most had long wings.

When *Pteranodon*'s wings were spread, they were about 8 yards (7.2 m) long. *Quetzalcoatlus* could spread its wings two times that far! No one knows how such big animals got into the air.

The First Birds

The first birds flew 150 million years ago. Birds came from the same group of reptiles as the dinosaurs. They may have come from *Compsognathus*. This dinosaur was the size of a hen. It was related to the larger ostrich dinosaurs.

Keeping Warm

Compsognathus was small. It used up its energy fast. But it didn't need to rest often, as most reptiles do. Somehow, it kept its body from cooling down quickly. *Compsognathus* may have been warm-blooded.

Scales covered the bodies of animals like *Compsognathus*. These scales may have held in heat. Maybe these scales split. The split ends joined. They held warm air next to the skin. Scales like these were the first true feathers.

Long-Ago Wings

Archaeopteryx was the first animal that was a true bird.

Its name means "ancient wings."

Archaeopteryx looked like a little dinosaur. It had teeth. Its tail was long and bony. Its arms had three fingers with claws.

It was different from a dinosaur in three ways: (1) toes that could hold onto a branch; (2) a bone that went around the hip (this bone pointed backwards); (3) wings with feathers.

Three *Archaeopteryx*. One is in the mud. Remains of birds like this have been found in West Germany. The bodies have changed to stone.

How the First Birds Flew

Some people think *Archaeopteryx* learned to fly by jumping. But most people who study animals think the first birds clawed their way up trees. Then they used their wings to glide down.

The wings of *Archaeopteryx* had feathers. These wings could not be hurt as easily as skin wings. Pterosaurs had skin wings.

Most likely, *Archaeopteryx* could not flap its wings hard enough to start flying. But by the end of the Dinosaur Age birds could fly well.

Crocodiles and Turtles

Crocodiles and turtles are two of the oldest groups of reptiles still alive. There were crocodiles and turtles more than 200 million years ago. Most crocodiles today live in pools and rivers. So did crocodiles in the Dinosaur Age. They swam well. On land they could run fast. They hid in the water and grabbed animals that came to drink.

Deinosuchus was a giant crocodile. It lived about 75 million years ago. It was about 16 yards (14.4 m) long. Its head was longer than a human's body. *Deinosuchus* may have grabbed big dinosaurs.

Heavy Shells

Today's tortoises have heavy shells. The first tortoises did too. They lived on land. Later some of these tortoises developed into turtles. These turtles had shells that were flat and light. Their feet were shaped like flippers. Some swam in pools and rivers. Others lived in the sea. They climbed to shore to lay their eggs.

Archelon was a huge sea turtle. It was about 4 yards (3.6 m) long. It lived about the same time as *Deinosuchus*. *Deinosuchus* was the biggest crocodile that ever lived. Turtles and crocodiles have not changed much since the days of *Deinosuchus*.

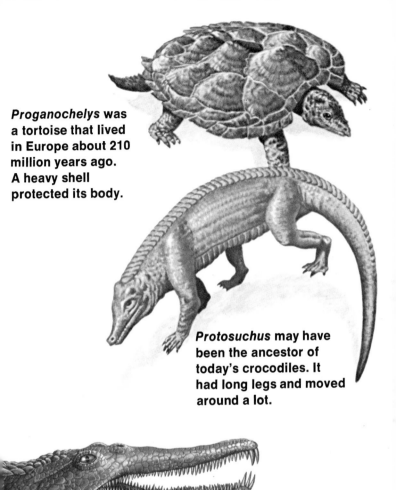

Proganochelys was a tortoise that lived in Europe about 210 million years ago. A heavy shell protected its body.

Protosuchus may have been the ancestor of today's crocodiles. It had long legs and moved around a lot.

Rutiodon was a *phytosaur*, which means "plant lizard." But phytosaurs did not eat plants. They had sharp teeth. They ate animals.

Fish Lizards

When dinosaurs ruled the land, big reptiles ruled the ocean. There were several kinds. At the start of the Dinosaur Age there were many **nothosaurs**. These looked like big lizards. But they had flat tails. Their sharp teeth snapped up fish.

At the same time **placodonts** ate shellfish on the seabed. Placodonts looked like short, thick nothosaurs. But their front teeth were shaped to grab and chew shellfish.

Nothosaurs and placodonts came to shore to lay eggs or have babies.

Ichthyosaurs swam fast enough to catch fish. They ate *ammonites* too. Ammonites are related to the octopus. But ammonites have coiled shells.

Fast Swimmers

The word *ichthyosaur* means "fish lizard." In early times ichthyosaurs swam faster than any other reptile. Ichthyosaurs grew to 11 yards (10 m) long. Their bodies were like those of today's dolphins.

Ichthyosaurs had thin snouts. They had sharp teeth to crunch their prey.

What Is Their Past?

Ichthyosaurs came from a reptile that lived on land. We do not know what kind of reptile it was. People study what is left of the oldest ichthyosaur they know about. It had a long, slim tail. This was not like the "fish" tail of later ichthyosaurs.

But this early ichthyosaur could not have moved on dry land. It was made for life in water. In fact, ichthyosaurs were born in water. But newborn babies had to swim quickly to the surface to breathe air.

Plesiosaurs

Nothosaurs died out early in the Dinosaur Age. But from them came a group that lasted a long time. These were swimming reptiles called **plesiosaurs**. Their name means "near lizards."

They had wider bodies than the nothosaurs. Their tails were short. Plesiosaurs had broad, flat flippers that they used as oars. The necks of some plesiosaurs were long. Others were short.

Long Necks

Someone wrote that a plesiosaur looked like a snake threaded through a turtle. These strange reptiles had short flippers and a long, thin neck. Their heads were small. A long-necked plesiosaur would swim with its head above water. When it saw a fish, its head went down after it.

These reptiles could not lift their flippers high. So they could not dive.

Pliosaurs

Pliosaurs were plesiosaurs with short necks. They had long flippers and strong jaws. They could swim faster and farther than the long-necked plesiosaurs. They dived to hunt for food.

Most of the time pliosaurs hunted relatives of the octopus. But *Kronosaurus* may have hunted long-necked plesiosaurs. *Kronosaurus* was about 19 yards (17.4 m) long.

A small pliosaur hunts for fish. A large plesiosaur. A flying pterosaur.

A small pliosaur

Elasmosaurus

Rhamphorhynchus

63

After the Dinosaurs

About 65 million years ago there were many dinosaurs. They lived much longer than humans have lived on earth. Dinosaurs died out long before the first human came. So did pterosaurs and big sea reptiles. No one knows why they died out.

Tyrannosaurus

Triceratops

Euoplocephalus

Parasaurolophus

Ornithomimus

Did They Kill Themselves?

Some dinosaurs ate flesh. Maybe they ate all of the other dinosaurs. Then they starved to death.

Some people say dinosaurs had such strange shapes that they could not breed.

Enemies?

Other people say that enemies killed the dinosaurs. Maybe small mammals ate their eggs. Or poisons may have grown on plants. Did dinosaurs eat the plants and die?

The Cold?

Maybe dinosaurs were drowned by floods. Or did gas from volcanoes poison them?

When dinosaurs died out, the world was getting cooler. People who study dinosaurs think they died because of the cold. They did not have hair to keep their bodies warm. They were too big to dig holes for themselves in the ground.

Rise of the Birds

Warm-blooded animals with fur or feathers could keep warm. So when the world got colder, birds and mammals did not die. Life was easier without dinosaurs hunting them.

Even while dinosaurs lived, there were new kinds of birds. Some birds started with *Archaeopteryx* (above). They still had teeth. They lived by the seas and hunted fish.

No Wings

Dinosaurs and big sea reptiles died out. Many birds no longer had to fly away from enemies. From these birds came many that could not fly. Giant penguins and giant pelicans hunted fish in the seas. Some birds that could not fly were taller than humans. They had strong beaks and claws. They lived on land. Most likely they hunted other animals. Other giant birds ate plants. Two of these were the giant moa of New Zealand and the elephant bird of Madagascar. They were like ostriches of today but much bigger.

This seabird is *Ichthyornis.* It is like a gull. It lived when pterosaurs were still alive. Birds flew better than pterosaurs. So pterosaurs died out. Big muscles helped the birds fly. Their chest bones jutted out. They helped hold the bird up. Arm and wrist bones made the wings strong.

Diatryma was taller than a human. It lived in North America 50 million years ago. It lived after the last dinosaurs died out. *Diatryma* had a strong beak and sharp claws. So *Diatryma* could win fights with most animals it met.

Creodonts were mammals that ate flesh. This creodont has found its food.

The Rise of Mammals

In the Dinosaur Age mammals were small and shy. After dinosaurs died out, there were bigger mammals. Some ate flesh. Others ate plants.

New Masters

The platypus and echidna came from an early group of mammals. These two mammals lay eggs.

A second group led to mammals with pouches. They are **marsupials**. Kangaroos are marsupials.

When marsupials are born, they are tiny. They crawl into a pouch in the mother's belly.

This second group of mammals led to **placental mammals** too. Cats and sheep are placental mammals. A **placenta** is part of the mother's body. It feeds the **fetus**. A fetus is the baby before it is born.

Dinosaurs were masters of the land 65 million years ago. Placental mammals have taken their place.

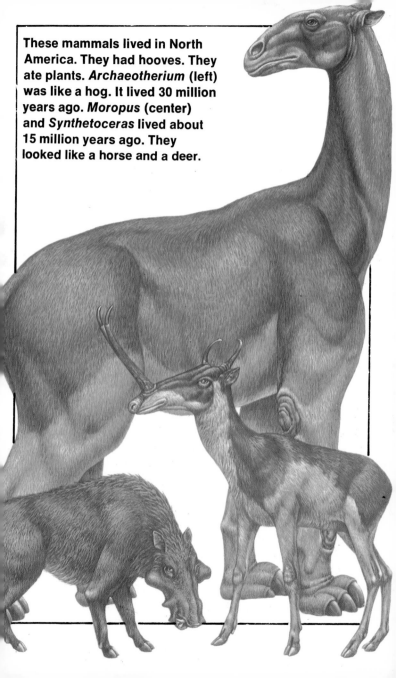

These mammals lived in North America. They had hooves. They ate plants. *Archaeotherium* (left) was like a hog. It lived 30 million years ago. *Moropus* (center) and *Synthetoceras* lived about 15 million years ago. They looked like a horse and a deer.

Four pictures show how a dinosaur became a fossil: (1) the body of a duck-billed dinosaur falls into the water; (2) mud covers the skeleton. As the bones rot, minerals take their place.

Dinosaur Fossils

Now mammals walk on lands that dinosaurs used to rule. What is left of dinosaurs' bodies lies in rocks. These remains are **fossils**. We found out everything we know about dinosaurs from their fossils.

For thousands of years people found fossils of plants and animals. People did not know how these fossils got into rocks. The Bible tells of a great flood. Did this flood wash fossils of sea shells onto the land?

About two hundred years ago James Hutton, a geologist from Scotland, studied how the earth began. He said fossils were buried in

the rocks while the rocks were being made.

Cemetery in the Sea

Millions and millions of plants and animals have died. Only a few of these have become fossils. Animals ate the rest. Or the bodies decayed. But some bodies fell to the bottom of a sea or lake. They were the most likely to become fossils. Mud or sand protected them.

Under Water

Sometimes a dinosaur drowned in river floods. Or it fell into the sea. Soft parts of its body rotted. Sometimes mud covered the bones fast. The mud kept the bones from rotting.

Hard things like bones, teeth, and shells are the most likely to become fossils.

How Fossils Are Made

What happened when mud piled up around a dinosaur in a seabed? Mud on top of the skeleton squashed the mud around it. The pressed mud turned to rock. While this was happening, water wore down the bones. Minerals in the water may have filled the spaces in the bones.

Maybe hard minerals, like silica, took the place of the bone. The bone was **petrified**. That means it turned to stone.

The earth's crust may have shifted, raising the rocks above the sea. Weather wore the rocks away. Only the fossil bones were left. If people did not save them, the fossils wore away too.

(3) Mud around a dinosaur fossil has turned to rock. The earth's crust moved. The rocks have been raised. Now they are on land.
(4) Weather has worn away the rock. The fossil is left.

71

Finding Dinosaurs

Hunting for dinosaur fossils is like the work of a detective. First hunters look for rocks that were made while dinosaurs were living. These rocks can only be found in certain areas. Then hunters look for places where rain has washed away the top soil, leaving the rocks bare. Fossil hunters walk slowly over these rocks. They study rocks that have fallen from cliffs. They study stones that water has washed down hills. Among these they may find bits of fossils. Then hunters know that fossils of skeletons may be in the rocks above.

Digging for Fossils

What happens when fossil hunters find a fossil dinosaur in a rock? First they must get it out. But the fossil may be on the side of a cliff. Or, perhaps most of it has fallen out and been washed away. The fossil hunters have to give up.

They may find a fossil worth digging out. Then a whole team of workers is needed. They may have to bulldoze or blow up tons of rock to get to the skeleton.

Next they use picks and shovels. They attack the rock around the bones. When they get down to the bones, they chip and scrape.

Before they get the bones all the way out, they put numbers on them. They take pictures. Later, people who work at museums must fit the bones together. The pictures and numbers help them.

Protecting Fossils

Some bones are very big. To get them out, workers may have to cut each bone into smaller pieces. They varnish the bones to protect them. They cover them with a lot of paper. They coat all of this with plaster of Paris. It gets hard. Thick splints of wood protect the whole thing.

A fossil *Iguanodon* was buried in these rocks. A fossil hunter uses a brush, hammer, pick, and other tools to get it out.

73

A Jigsaw Puzzle

A museum gets the fossil dinosaur. Many months pass before it is ready to be shown.

Workers soak off the paper that covers the fossil. They chip away any stone around the bones. The workers may use power tools to speed up their work. One tool works like a dentist's drill. Another tool blows out sand in a jet of air. It blasts rock away from the fossil bone.

They Study the Bones

The fossil bones are cleaned. Then, they are studied. How did the bones fit together when the dinosaur was alive?

Finding this out can be hard. The photographs help. But animals may have pulled some bones apart after the dinosaur died. Water from floods may have mixed up the bones.

Building the Body

Putting the bones in place is like a jigsaw puzzle. Metal rods and clamps are used to join the bones. The bones have marks that show where muscles joined the bones. Workers fix the skeleton so it stands as the dinosaur used to stand.

No one knows the color of dinosaurs for sure. Most likely their color was like things around them. That would have helped them hide from enemies.

How Dinosaurs Lived

People who study fossil dinosaurs learn a lot about what they looked like. And they learn how dinosaurs lived. Bones of the legs show how dinosaurs walked. The teeth tell if they ate flesh or leaves. Holes in the skull tell what kind of brains, eyes, nose, and ears the animals had.

But there are still some puzzles.

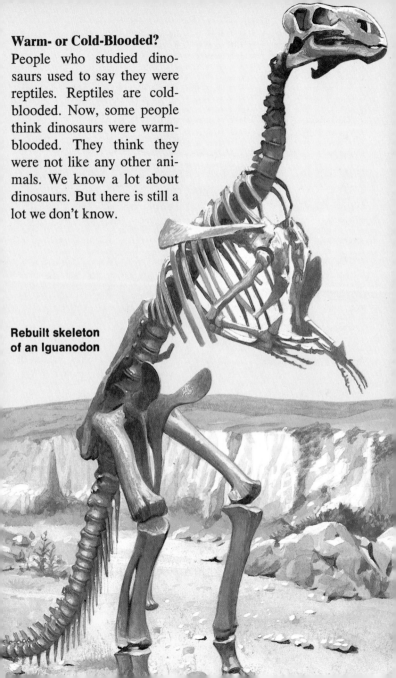

Warm- or Cold-Blooded?

People who studied dinosaurs used to say they were reptiles. Reptiles are cold-blooded. Now, some people think dinosaurs were warm-blooded. They think they were not like any other animals. We know a lot about dinosaurs. But there is still a lot we don't know.

Rebuilt skeleton of an Iguanodon

Do You Know?

Big and Small

Most dinosaurs were giants. But some were smaller than a human. *Compsognathus* was about the size of a hen. This picture shows sizes of five dinosaurs, a pterosaur, a car, and a man.

Heavy and Light

Brachiosaurus weighed about 100 tons (90.7 metric tons). This was more than 1400 people weigh.

Apatosaurus (also named *Brontosaurus*) was a sauropod. It weighed about 30 tons (27.2 metric tons). This was as much as 428 people. Three *Tyrannosauruses* weighed as much as one *Apatosaurus.*

Triceratops weighed 8.5 tons. *Stegoceras* was even lighter. Four *Pteranodons* weighed only as much as one person.

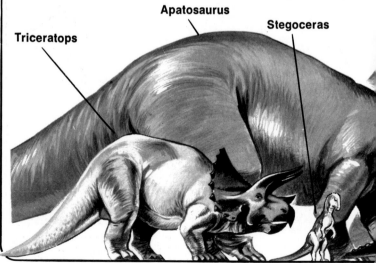

Apatosaurus

Stegoceras

Triceratops

Pteranodon

Brachiosaurus

Tyrannosaurus

77

Big Finds

Sometimes many fossil bones have been found in one place. And fossil bones have been found where people did not expect them. These bones have helped us learn a lot about dinosaurs.

In 1878 coal miners in Belgium found a fossil herd. Workers dug up about thirty-one fossil *Iguanodons*! For the first time people who studied *Iguanodons* learned what they looked like.

A Missing Link

In 1969 the remains of a *Lystrosaurus* (shown below) was found in Antarctica.

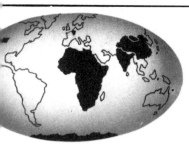

Above: Areas in black show fossil finds around the world

Lystrosaurus was a reptile about the size of a sheep. It lived more than 200 million years ago in Africa, India, and China. It could not have swum across the sea to Antarctica. This showed that some continents were joined together when the Dinosaur Age began. Now these continents are far away from each other.

Fights of Long Ago

A few fossil finds show one dinosaur attacking or eating another. The American Museum of Natural History in New York City has a skeleton of a brontosaur. Its tail shows teeth marks of *Allosaurus. Allosaurus* teeth were found near the fossil tail.

In 1971 fossil hunters in Mongolia found fossils of two dinosaurs. They died while fighting each other. One was *Velociraptor.* It ate flesh. When it died, its arms and legs held the head of a *Protoceratops.*

Footprints and Eggs

Fossil bones are not the only things that tell us about life in the Dinosaur Age. We can learn from other kinds of dinosaur fossils. There are fossils of their eggs, footprints, droppings, and even what's left over from meals.

Human footprints and dinosaur footprints

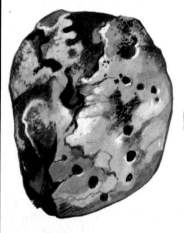

A Mosasaur's Meal

Above we see the fossil of an ammonite. A young **mosasaur** bit the ammonite sixteen times. A mosasaur is a giant sea lizard.

Giant Footprints

Sometimes dinosaurs left footprints in wet mud. The mud dried. It got hard and became rock. These fossil footprints tell us about animals that walked millions of years ago.

Sauropods had feet the size of big bass drums.

One set of sauropod footprints showed only the front feet. The animal had been swimming. Its back feet were up.

Very Old Eggs

In the 1920s Ray Chapman Andrews, an American, led a group of people to the deserts of Mongolia. They went to look for fossils. They found nests of eggs like those shown here. Some eggs had been smashed. Others held fossils of babies. These babies had died before they had time to hatch. The dinosaur *Protoceratops* laid the eggs.

In 1961 fossil hunters in France found sauropod eggs. They were 80 million years old. They were two times the size of today's ostrich eggs. We don't know of any eggs that are bigger.

Freaks

Not all fossils were made when minerals took the place of bones. Some fossils were just holes left in rocks when water wore the bones away.

Some fossils were formed in ice, tar, or other material.

Frozen Mammoths
Mammoths (like the one shown above) were similar to the elephants of

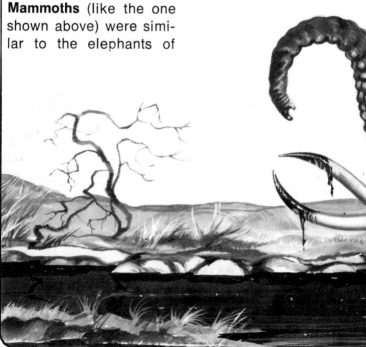

today. They died out thousands of years ago. Many were buried when frozen soil slid down slopes. The soil stayed frozen, so the bodies of some mammoths did not decay. They still have hair and flesh.

In the last 250 years people have found remains of 117,000 mammoths in Siberia. Others were found in North America and Europe.

Tar Traps

There are pools of tar near Los Angeles, California. About 15,000 years ago animals tried to drink rainwater that was on the tar. Many animals sank into the sticky pools. The animals died. The tar around their bodies got hard.

People have found bones of bison, horses, and mammoths in the tar pits.

Fossil Hunters

Fossil hunters of the 1800s taught us a lot about the Dinosaur Age. These two pages tell about four hunters and the fossils they found.

Mary Anning

Mary Anning

Mary Anning (1799–1847) lived in southern England. She lived near sea cliffs. She dug up many fossils from the Dinosaur Age. When Mary was eleven, she found the first full skeleton of an ichthyosaur.

Gideon Mantell

Dr. Mantell (1790–1852) lived in England. In 1822 his wife found fossil teeth in a rock. They made Mantell think of the teeth of an iguana lizard. So he said the teeth came from "*Iguanodon*." This means "iguana tooth."

In 1841 a British scientist thought of the name *dinosaur* for *Iguanodon* and animals like it. Dinosaur means "terrible lizard."

Gideon Mantell

Othniel Marsh

Edward Drinker Cope

Edward Drinker Cope (1840–1897) studied animals of the North American West. He studied backboned animals that had died out.

Cope and Marsh liked to see who could find the most fossils. Cope and his workers found nine new kinds of fossil dinosaurs. Most of his dinosaurs are in the American Museum of Natural History in New York City.

Othniel Marsh

Othniel Marsh (1831–1899) was a **paleontologist**. That means he was trained to study fossils. He was an American.

Marsh taught at a museum. He sent teams of fossil hunters to look for remains of animals.

Tons of fossil bones were sent to him from states in the West. He found more new kinds of fossil dinosaurs than anyone else.

Edward Drinker Cope

Dinosaurs That Never Were

After dinosaurs died, there were no more animals that looked like them. So, the first people who found dinosaur fossils did not know how to fit the bones together. Sometimes, they made big mistakes!

Iguanodon had thumbs that were like spikes. Hawkins found only one fossil thumb. He thought the snout was the right place for it.

Strange Monsters

Benjamin Waterhouse Hawkins lived in London. The picture shows his workshop in 1835.

Hawkins made life-size models of early animals. He made them for a park. Some of his monsters are still at the park.

Hawkins did not know how the real animals looked. His *Iguanodon* is the animal in the center. It looks like a giant rhinoceros with four legs. But the real *Iguanodon* had two legs. And it had no horn.

Heads or Tails?

In 1868 American fossil hunters found the fossil of a swimming reptile. These hunters were working for Edward Drinker Cope.

Cope named the plesiosaur *Elasmosaurus*. Cope said it was not like any other reptile.

It was put in a museum in Philadelphia. Professor Joseph Leidy saw that something was wrong. He took away the last bone that Cope had put on the tail. Leidy put it on the head where it belonged!

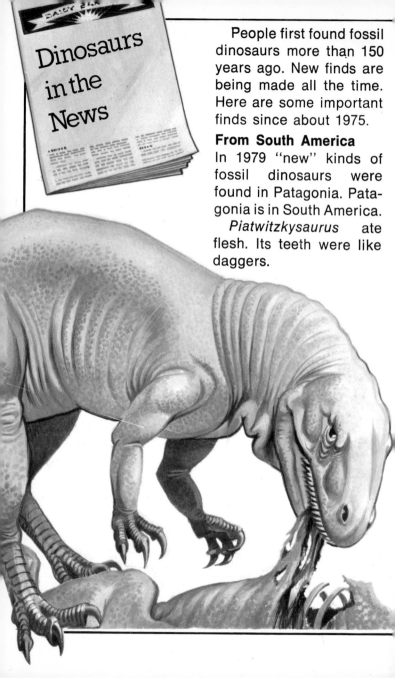

Dinosaurs in the News

People first found fossil dinosaurs more than 150 years ago. New finds are being made all the time. Here are some important finds since about 1975.

From South America

In 1979 "new" kinds of fossil dinosaurs were found in Patagonia. Patagonia is in South America.

Piatwitzkysaurus ate flesh. Its teeth were like daggers.

SOUTH AMERICA

Patagonia

Patagosaurus and *Volk-heimeria* were big sauropods. They ate plants.

These dinosaurs lived more than 135 million years ago. They are different from North American dinosaurs.

Family Life
Some people who study dinosaurs say they took care of their young. Others say dinosaurs laid their eggs and left.

In 1979 American fossil hunters in Montana found a dip in the ground. In it were fossil skeletons of eleven baby dinosaurs. They were duckbills. They were just hatched when they died.

Some of their bones had not grown hard. The babies were too young to leave the nest to find food. But they had used their teeth. This showed that the parents may have brought them food.

Strong Swimmers
In 1980 dinosaur tracks were found in the dry bed of an old lake. The tracks were more than 150 million years old. They showed that some two-legged dinosaurs that ate flesh could swim. One track showed that the claw and tip of each middle toe hit bottom first. Then outer claws scraped back as the animal kicked through the water.

Still Here

Not many kinds of animals last more than a few million years. Most animals that lived in the Dinosaur Age have gone. But some have stayed.

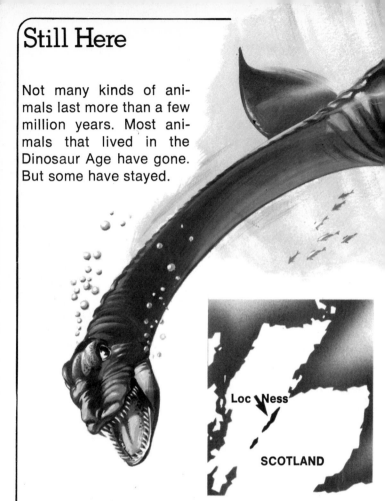

Loc Ness

SCOTLAND

Lake Monsters
Many people say they have seen mounds rise out of Loch Ness. Loch Ness is a lake in Scotland. Other people say they have seen a long neck in Loch Ness. Maybe there are still plesiosaurs in deep lakes. But no one has caught a plesiosaur. So, we can't say for sure that such an animal is in Loch Ness.

Coelacanth

King Crab
King crabs live in the sea. They are not really crabs. They are the only living relatives of **trilobites**. Trilobites died out about 250 million years ago.

Look Who's Here!
Coelacanths are lobe-finned fish. People thought they died out 70 million years ago. But in 1938 a living one was found. Since then many have been found.

Index